YER

Lisa Thompson

First published in the UK 2010 by
A & C Black Publishing Ltd
36 Soho Square
London
W1D 3QY
www.acblack.com

Copyright © 2009 Blake Publishing
Published 2008 by Blake Education Pty Ltd, Australia

ISBN: 978-1-4081-2873-2

Written by Lisa Thompson and Elizabeth Dowen
Editor: Emma Waterhouse
Photo research: Anna Di Losa and Sandra Iannella
Cover Design: Cliff Watt
Designer: D Brown and Clifford Hayes
Printed and bound in China by Leo Paper Products.

Cover image © shutterstock/Yuri Arcurs

All images © Shutterstock except pp10-11(diagram) "Who's Who in the
Courtroom" © Courts Service of Ireland; p18(bl) (br), p 19(bl) (bm),
p 29(br), p 34(bl) (br)–Corbis; p 20(t)–courtesy of the US Library of
Congress, LC-USF3301-001112-M1; p 20(b) – courtesy of the US Library
of Congress, LC–USW3-037973-E; p 21(mr), p 35(b)–AAP

With grateful thanks to Amy Brown and Jonathan Marquet for their generous
assistance.

New Message   Get Mail   Reply   Reply All   Forward   Note   To

MAILBOXES

Inbox

Mail files_Clien

Mail files_Hom

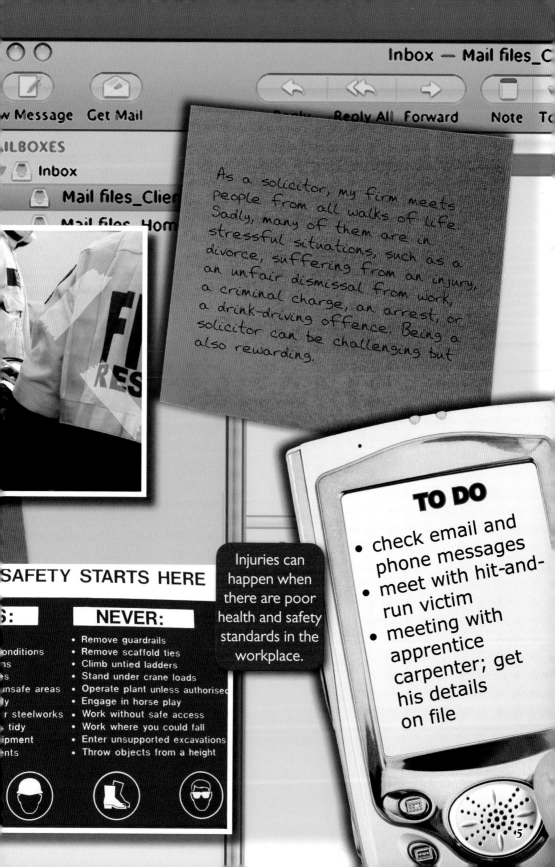

As a solicitor, my firm meets people from all walks of life. Sadly, many of them are in stressful situations, such as a divorce, suffering from an injury, an unfair dismissal from work, a criminal charge, an arrest, or a drink-driving offence. Being a solicitor can be challenging but also rewarding.

TO DO

- check email and phone messages
- meet with hit-and-run victim
- meeting with apprentice carpenter; get his details on file

SAFETY STARTS HERE

Injuries can happen when there are poor health and safety standards in the workplace.

S:

NEVER:

conditions
ns
es
unsafe areas
ly
r steelworks
tidy
ipment
ents

- Remove guardrails
- Remove scaffold ties
- Climb untied ladders
- Stand under crane loads
- Operate plant unless authorised
- Engage in horse play
- Work without safe access
- Work where you could fall
- Enter unsupported excavations
- Throw objects from a height

5

Annabel calls

11 am – My colleague, Annabel Martin, calls me from the District Court. She spends most of her time appearing there and she's currently representing one of our clients who was injured in a car accident. The other driver was at fault and now faces criminal charges for dangerous driving. He is due for his pre-trial court appearance today.

Annabel tells me the defendant has not shown up for court, which means that the trial cannot proceed today.

We're keen for the trial to go ahead as quickly as possible, so we make our way over to the courthouse to plead our case to the judge. We ask that he set a date for the trial to proceed and luckily, the judge agrees with us — the trial date is set.

The trial date is set

All this has happened and it's only lunchtime!

SUMMONS
TO APPEAR

good communication skills

strong research skills

DID YOU KNOW?

What's in a word?

A lawyer is a person who has a law degree and a licence to practise law. The word *lawyer* means different things in different countries. In Australia, the word *lawyer* refers to both *solicitors* and *barristers*. In America, lawyers are also known as *attorneys*. In England and Wales, *lawyer* means a variety of law-trained persons. It includes *barristers*, *solicitors*, *legal executives* and *judges*. This book looks at working as a solicitor.

QUALITIES NEEDED TO BE A GOOD SOLICITOR:

• an ability to identify, analyse and solve complex problems

• the capacity to think through large amounts of written information

• critical thinking skills

• good communication skills

• an ability to handle confidential information privately

• planning and organisational skills

• professional personal presentation

• strong reading and research skills

• an ability to work in a professional and ethical manner

• an ability to work independently and in a team

• the capacity to work in a practical and orderly manner.

teamwork

how i became a solicitor

I took English, history and politics A levels and did work experience in a legal firm. Shadowing a solicitor dealing with young offenders, he explained the importance of communication skills, being able to listen carefully and ask the right questions.

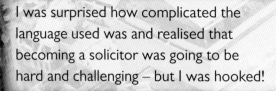

I was surprised how complicated the language used was and realised that becoming a solicitor was going to be hard and challenging – but I was hooked!

I needed really good exam results and also had to sit the LNAT (National Admissions Test for Law) exams to go to the University of Birmingham to read Law. The LNAT helps universities choose from hundreds of applicants, so I was lucky to get a place!

After university I managed to get a two-year trainee contract with a solicitor's office. I gained valuable experience working on different cases early in my career. After 12 months of practical experience I had to pass the PSC (Professional Skills Course) to finally qualify. It was a long road, but it was worthwhile.

Most cases we work on deal with criminal law, family law and claims for compensation. Regardless of whether you work in a small or a large firm, in the country or the city, people should have access to excellent legal representation.

At the moment I specialise in personal injury claims and eventually I hope to be a partner in the firm.

Red-hot fact!

For hundreds of years headgear of some kind has been worn in court. The word wig is short for periwig, derived from the French word for a wig, perruque.

WHO'S WHO IN THE COURTROOM

At court, you might see the following people:

Judge – The judge is in charge in the courtroom and gives the jury any advice they need.

Court Reporter – The court reporter types up everything that is said in the case.

Witness – The prosecution and/or defence call witnesses to prove their case. Barristers cross-examine witnesses to see whether their evidence is accurate.

Witness

Court Reporter

Barrister – Barristers present the case in court. Barristers for the prosecution are called counsel for the prosecution. Barristers for the accused are called counsel for the defence.

Solicitor

Accused

Barrister

Accused – The accused sits before the court, accused of committing a crime.

Prison officer

DID YOU KNOW?

OLDEST
In North America, the oldest serving federal judge was Joseph W. Woodrough. He worked as a senior judge at the U.S. Court of Appeals, until he died at 104 years of age.

— A CRIMINAL CASE

Judge

Registrar/Court clerk – They assist the judge with administration, such as calling the names of jurors, looking after documents and exhibits, and recording the names of witnesses.

Registrar/Court clerk

Solicitor – Solicitors meet with clients and prepare a case for trial. They get all the documents ready and instruct the barrister, who will present the case.

Solicitor

Members of the public

12 people = a jury

A jury consists of 12 members of the community, with no legal training and no previous connection to the case. The community randomly selects members of the jury for each case. A jury decides the guilt or innocence of an accused person. Sometimes, a jury's decision of guilt or innocence must be unanimous.
For other cases, only a majority of jurors need to agree.

Jury – The jury hears the evidence and decides whether the accused is guilty or innocent.

WHAT IS A SOLICITOR?

Solicitors work as lawyers in a range of different organisations – private practices, government departments or providing legal assistance to people who can't afford to pay for it.

Solicitors prepare their case for trial.

Some solicitors work as sole practitioners in private practices or in partnership with other solicitors at large law firms. Other solicitors, who work in small firms like mine, deal with wills and estates, small offences and family law matters.

WHAT IS A LEGAL EXECUTIVE?

In England and Wales, Legal executives are qualified lawyers, specialising in particular areas of law like conveyancing or family law. They have at least five years' experience working under the supervision of a solicitor.

They have their own client files and their work is charged directly to the client. This is an important difference between legal executives and other legal support staff. Legal executives undertake a series of training courses and are required to pass qualifications in Law in the area of legal practice that they intend to specialise. Trainees will often work at the same time as studying in order to acquire practical skills.

Corporate solicitors make sure companies don't break the law.

WHAT IS A BARRISTER?

Barristers give advice on certain areas of the law. The solicitor first briefs the barrister on the details of the case, and the barrister then speaks in court on the client's behalf.

Asking for counsel

For my workers compensation case, I ask barrister Matthew Graham for his advice. He and I will prepare the case together, but he will represent my client in court. To prepare our case, we research previous workers compensation cases. Studying this information will help us to see how judges have ruled in the past.

WHAT IS A QC?

These were barristers appointed in the late 16th century to help the law officers of the crown in the conduct of legal affairs. They are said to 'take silk' on appointment, as they then wear a silk gown instead of a 'stuff' gown. A small number of senior barristers are made Queen's Counsel these days as a mark of outstanding ability. They are normally work on serious or complex cases.

DIDYOUKNOW?

First female

Helena Normanton was the first woman to be admitted as a barrister in England, in 1922. She then went on to be the first woman to prosecute someone for murder, conduct a trial in America and to represent cases at the High Court and the Old Bailey.

Certain organisations give legal advice at low or no cost to people in need.

Different lawyers for different laws

MANY OF MY FRIENDS ARE SOLICITORS.
HERE ARE A FEW AREAS THEY SPECIALISE IN:

CONTRACT

Corporate lawyers have to check a lot of contracts.

Corporate law

Corporate lawyers, like my friend Will, supervise commercial agreements between companies. The lawyers make sure these agreements are legal and that the companies don't break the law.

Employment and Workplace law

Employment lawyers advise employees and employers about legal issues in the workplace, such as health and safety standards. Big law firms usually advise employers, while smaller firms often represent employees.

Family law

Family lawyers handle cases to do with child custody, divorce and property settlements.

A solicitor's 'to do' list

A solicitor may perform the following tasks:

- ✓ draft legal documents
- ✓ interview clients
- ✓ write letters on behalf of clients
- ✓ negotiate on behalf of clients
- ✓ research the law
- ✓ write legal advice
- ✓ prepare documents for court.

1

Employers need to look after their employees.

entertainment law

As an entertainment lawyer, my friend Renee advises and represents people who work in the entertainment industry. This includes people who work in television, sport, music, film, theatre, print and media advertising. Cases may involve copyright issues and personality rights.

Musicians copyright their music.

New technology means the entertainment industry is always changing.

Photographers may own the rights to their photos. That means anyone who wishes to use these photos has to buy them from the photographer.

immigration lawyers

Every country has different immigration laws. Immigration lawyers, like my friend Cris, advise people who want to become citizens of a country, or want to live and work temporarily in a new country.

a well-travelled passport

for different laws

criminal law

Tyson's always on call.

Manuscripts are protected under copyright law.

SCREENPLAY

VINCI 6d

SANDA ISL

16

riminal law

Criminal lawyers defend people who are accused of breaking the law. As a criminal lawyer, my friend Tyson handles cases ranging from murder and internet fraud to drink-driving charges.

ntellectual property

Intellectual property lawyers deal with issues concerning patents, industrial designs, fine art works and copyright of written works, films and images.

One of my colleagues, Jo, works as a patent lawyer. Patent law is one type of intellectual property law. It protects people who invent products from other people who might use the products illegally.

Copyright law is another type of intellectual property law. It protects people from having their written works, music, artwork or other creations copied illegally.

Real estate

Real estate lawyers specialise in issues to do with land and property, such as mortgages, leases and homes for sale.

Personal injury

As a personal injury lawyer, my friend Rami works on cases where someone has been injured due to another person or a business' negligence.

There are many other areas to specialise in. Here are just a few:

- Banking & finance law
- Construction law
- Environmental law
- EU & competition law
- Human rights law
- IT & communications law
- Life sciences law
- Shipping law

DID YOU KNOW?

Online music is everywhere. But a lot of the music that is downloaded is not from a legal store and is unlicensed, and the people who make it available are breaking the law.

Most music is protected by copyright. Recordings are in copyright for 50 years in the UK even if the music is much older. Much of the music you find online is legally protected by copyright law so you need a licence to copy it!

File-sharing, Peer to Peer (P2P) and downloading can also be illegal. More information can be found at www.pro-music.org.

drafting a will

Lawyers help you go over things in detail.

THE LAW IN HISTORY

THERE ARE MANY IMPORTANT MILESTONES IN THE HISTORY OF LAW.

HAMMURABI'S CODE

Hammurabi's Code is the best preserved ancient law code that exists today. King Hammurabi made the Code around 1760 BC, in ancient Babylon. He believed the gods chose him to deliver the law to his people. It is the earliest-known example of a ruler publicly giving his subjects a set of laws to follow. The code was carved on a black, stone monument that stood two metres tall. Only one part exists today.

BABYLON

Hammurabi's Code

MAGNA CARTA

In 1215, King John of England was forced to sign the *Magna Carta* to appease his subjects. Magna Carta is Latin for *Great Paper*, and was the first legal document that made an English monarch accountable to the law. The King no longer had unlimited power and was forced to follow certain legal procedures. The Magna Carta ultimately influenced many constitutional documents, such as the United States Constitution.

A painting of King John signing the Magna Carta.

The Triangle Shirtwaist Factory Fire

The Triangle Shirtwaist Factory fire, in 1911, was the largest workplace disaster in the history of New York City. Though many of the workers got out of the building in time, there weren't enough fire escapes and about 146 workers died. Ultimately, Max Blanck and Isaac Harris, the company's owners, were found *not guilty* on manslaughter charges. They were later convicted of negligence in a civil case and had to pay compensation to the victims' families. The fire led to new laws improving factory safety standards and workers compensation rights.

Firefighters try to put out the fire.

DIDYOUKNOW?

MULTI TALENTED

BESIDES BEING AN ARTIST AND AN INVENTOR, LEONARDO DA VINCI WAS ALSO A LAWYER!

Modern safety regulations require buildings to have proper fire escapes.

EXIT

Segregation laws overturned

1865 – The Jim Crow laws in America prevented African-Americans and other non-white racial groups from attending certain public schools and using certain facilities, such as restaurants, theatres, hotels, cinemas, trains and buses.

1896 – Judge John Harlan of the Supreme Court said it was wrong to keep African-Americans legally inferior to white people.

1954 – In the *Brown v Board of Education* case, the Supreme Court ruled that separate public schools for African-American and white students denied African-American children equal education opportunities.

1964 – Congress passed the *Civil Rights Act*. This established equal employment opportunities for white and African-American people, and made racial discrimination illegal in public places.

1965 – Congress passed the *Voting Rights Act*. This made discrimination in voting illegal and allowed millions of African-Americans to vote for the first time.

1967 – President Lyndon Baines Johnson nominated a civil rights attorney, Thurgood Marshall, to be the first African-American Associate Justice of the Supreme Court.

African Americans and white Americans had separate water bubblers.

They also had separate waiting rooms at train stations.

The Old Bailey

The Old Bailey is the Central Criminal Court in London where major cases are heard. It stands on the site of a medieval jail. Above the main entrance is inscribed 'Defend the Children of the Poor & Punish the Wrongdoer'.

The oldest courts of the Old Bailey are number one, two and three and it is here that a great many infamous people have stood trial. Public hangings here stopped in 1868. Thousands of people gathered to watch the executions and many rented rooms in nearby houses.

Trials in the Old Bailey are open to the public but it is forbidden to take any notes or to use cameras or mobile phones.

Famous trials at The Old Bailey

- Lord Haw Haw was tried for treason after WWII.

- The Kray Brothers, London gangsters, were tried at the Old Bailey

- The Yorkshire Ripper's reign of terror came to an end in the famous Court No.1.

DID YOU KNOW?

The television series Rumpole of the Bailey is about a defence lawyer who works at the Bailey.

Lawyer speak

Lawyers often sound like they speak a foreign language, so it's important to make sure our clients understand exactly what we're talking about.

Bona Fide – This means a person is acting honestly, genuinely and sincerely in the absence of fraud, wrongdoing or deception.

Affidavit – A statement, signed before a solicitor or barrister. The person signing the legal document states that the contents are true, to the best of their knowledge.

Bail – A written commitment or promise to appear in court when required. Bail conditions might require the accused to stay away from people involved in the case, or report to the police to show that they have not left the country.

Cross-examination – When a barrister on the opposing side questions a witness or the defendant about details to do with the case.

Brief – A written list of the evidence, such as witness statements, photographs and test results, or anything lawyers will use to argue the case.

Evidence – Information and facts about the crime scene, such as physical evidence, like fingerprints, or information about the defendant that lawyers use in court.

Plea – The defendant's answer to a charge, usually *guilty* or *not guilty*. This is read out when the defendant first appears in court.

Prosecutor – A trial lawyer who represents the government in a criminal case.

Voir Dire – This refers to a "trial within a trial". It is a hearing to determine the admissibility of evidence, or the competency of a witness or juror.

Subpoena – A court order requesting that a witness brings documents to court and/or give evidence at court. This is often called a witness summons.

At some time, almost everyone needs a lawyer.

23

Decision Making

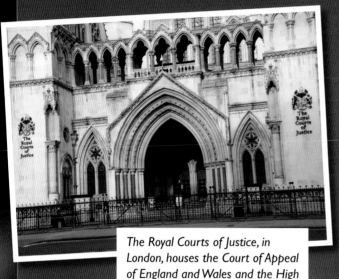

The Royal Courts of Justice, in London, houses the Court of Appeal of England and Wales and the High Court of Justice of England

In both criminal and civil cases, the prosecution and defence try to prove to the court that they are right and the other side is wrong.

In **criminal cases** a jury decides whether they are guilty, and the judge issues their sentence.

In **civil and family cases**, the judge decides who is right based on the evidence presented.

Different courts in England and Wales

The choice of court depends in most cases on the value of the claim.

The Supreme Court is the highest appeal court in almost all cases in England and Wales.

Court of Appeal of England and Wales hears cases in which lower courts have made decisions, but now those involved in the case disagree with what has been decided.

Crown Court deal with more serious criminal cases, such as murder, rape or robbery. Trials are heard by a judge and a 12-person jury. Members of the public are selected for jury service.

High Court of Justice (Queen's Bench, Chancery and Family division) deals with claims of over a value of £25,000.

Crown courtroom, Liverpool

High Court of Justice (Queen's Bench, Chancery and Family division) deals with claims of over a value of £25,000.

Magistrates Court deal with less serious criminal cases and civil matters. Magistrates determining whether a defendant is guilty or not, and pass. They do not use a jury but instead three magistrates sitting as a 'bench' to decide and pass judgement on the person who is accused of the crime.

County Court cases are mostly between people or companies who believe that someone owes them money. This includes claims for debts, personal injury, divorce or adoption and housing disputes.

Different courts in Scotland

1. **The Court of Session** is the supreme civil court in Scotland, based in Edinburgh.

2. **The Sheriff Court** is the local court and there are 49 sheriff courts across Scotland. The sheriff courts deal with the majority of civil cases

3. **Tribunals** also sit in Scotland, covering a wide range of subjects including employment, education, children's hearings, social security and tax.

CHILDREN IN COURT

Most countries around the world believe that children who are charged with committing a crime should not be tried in court as adults. This means that members of the court must follow certain rules.

During my work experience at the *Young Offenders' Legal Hotline*, I learnt about the different rules that protect children in criminal cases.

1. The United Nations Convention on the Rights of the Child says how young people should be treated when they get into trouble.

2. If the person is under 18 in England and Wales, their case may be held in Youth Court (part of the Magistrates Court). These are less formal than magistrates' courts, and the judges do not wear robes.

3. In Scotland, eight-year-olds can face prosecution. The majority are dealt with by Children's Panels until the age of 16.

✓ Red-hot fact!

Ages of criminal responsibility

US (some states): 6
Scotland: 8
England, Wales and Northern Ireland: 10
Australia: 10
Canada, Netherlands: 12
France: 13
Germany, Austria, Italy, Japan, Russia: 14
Denmark, Norway and Sweden: 15
Spain, Portugal: 16
Brazil, Peru: 18

DIDYOUKNOW?

How Old?

Almost 3,000 crimes in England and Wales were reported in 2006 where the suspect was too young to be prosecuted.

It's often very stressful for parents.

THE LAW

At 13 you can...
- get a part-time job – you can do 'light' work, which means jobs that don't affect your health, safety or education – jobs like babysitting or paper rounds.

At 14 you can...
- be held responsible for a crime
- give evidence
- be responsible for wearing a seatbelt – that's right, it's not just the driver's responsibility. If you get caught not wearing one you could be fined.

KIDS' COURT

Trial proceedings in a Children's Court are less formal. The court tries to make sure that the child understands what happens in a court trial and that they are able to give their testimony.

At 16 you can...
- change your name by Deed Poll as long as you have parental consent.
- buy a pet without an adult being with you
- drink wine, beer or cider with a meal
- fly a glider

CHILDREN WORLDWIDE

Since World War II, countries have made significant laws to protect children. Countries such as Argentina, Israel, Japan and Greece have established laws to protect:
- children's health
- a child's right to education
- children from abuse and exploitation
- children's rights in the legal system.

At 17 you can...
- donate blood
- be sent to an adult prison
- leave home without your parents' consent
- hold an air pilot's licence

At 18 you can...
- get a tattoo
- vote in local, national and European elections
- get married without consent or register a civil partnership
- stand to become an MP

Breaking
THE LAW

Many people assume that all solicitors either defend or prosecute people who have broken the law.

There are actually two types of law-breaking:

✗ Under civil law – when one person has harmed another but it's not a crime, such as a broken contract. In this case, the person who has suffered the damage may bring an action against the other person to sue them for damages.

✗ Under criminal law – when someone commits a crime, for example murder or fraud. In this case, the police or government can bring an action against the person for them to be punished.

DIDYOUKNOW?

Legal systems

The legal systems in England, Wales and Northern Ireland are almost the same. Scotland uses other names and is arranged differently but it works in a similar way to the legal system in England and Wales.

✓ Red-hot fact!

The law in England and Wales is made in two very different ways:

Case Law is the oldest type of law making and is based upon Norman practice, when there used to be travelling courts which tried cases and made decisions which were then followed by other courts.

Statute Law or Common Law is laid down by parliament, and it is superior to case law. It comes from an Act of Parliament.

What happens when a crime is committed

Offence and complaint to the police

Police investigate and take statements

Crown Prosecution Service (CPS) decides the charge

Bail considered

Hearing in Court

Indictable matters (serious)

Non-indictable matters (less serious)

Proceedings before a magistrate

Magistrate hears plea, evidence, decides outcome

Dismisses matter, accused set free

Trial in Crown Court

Not Guilty plea

Conviction

Guilty plea

Possible appeal against conviction

Trial date set

Accused is sentenced

Trial before judge and jury or judge alone

Guilty and sentenced

Not guilty, accused goes free

Possible appeal against conviction

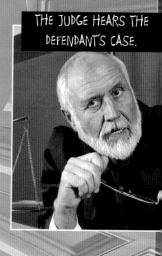

THE JUDGE HEARS THE DEFENDANT'S CASE.

THE TRIAL PROCEEDINGS ARE UNDERWAY.

YOU ARE UNDER ARREST!

POWERS OF ARREST

If police officers reasonably suspect that a person has committed, or is about to commit, a crime they can arrest that person. However, police officers should only use arrest as a last resort. Resisting arrest is a serious offence. If the police arrest someone who is involved in their investigation, that person should voluntarily cooperate with the police.

PREPARING A CRIMINAL CASE

For a criminal case, after I've read the list of charges against my client, the next thing I do is draw up a case plan. The case plan includes a list of all the relevant documents, statements and a list of witnesses. My team and I will need these to help us build our case.

These documents may include:

- a brief of evidence
- police statements
- client statements
- witness statements
- tests (if relevant), e.g. blood or DNA tests
- statements from specialists, e.g. doctors
- evidence lists from the crime scene.

Taped conversations may be admitted as evidence.

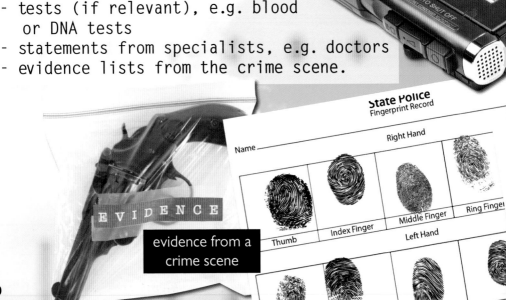

evidence from a crime scene

State Police
Fingerprint Record

Name

Right Hand

Thumb   Index Finger   Middle Finger   Ring Finger

Left Hand

Middle Finger   Index F

A BRIEF OF EVIDENCE

If the defendant appearing in court pleads not guilty, the police and CPS (Crown Prosecution Service) prepare a brief of evidence. A brief of evidence contains all the written statements, charges and exhibits that the prosecution uses to argue their case against the defendant. This includes anything that the defendant has said.

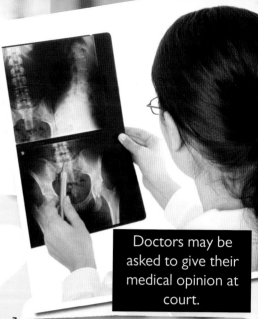

Doctors may be asked to give their medical opinion at court.

Exhibits are pieces of physical evidence that police collect from a crime scene, such as clothing, footprints or blood. Sometimes, forensic scientists will examine the crime scene or evidence and give their expert opinion on these things in court. The defendant's solicitor analyses the brief of evidence to build a case that will prove their client's innocence.

BACK AND FORTH

The judge can look at a case a number of times before he or she decides that enough evidence has been gathered for it to go to trial.

Surveillance footage – was the suspect caught on camera?

Witnesses may have to testify as to what they saw at a crime scene.

Blood alcohol tests could prove the accused was driving dangerously.

Updates on my cases

HIT-AND-RUN — WITNESS TESTIMONIES

Barrister, Sarah Charleston, has agreed to represent my client in court. We look over the brief of evidence to prepare for our court appearance. The brief of evidence contains statements from three witnesses. Hopefully this evidence will help to convict the defendant. The witnesses are a man who owns a corner store across from where the accident occurred, an old lady who was walking her dog and a young boy who was playing with a ball nearby.

The statements describe what these three people saw — the colour of the car that hit my client, what the driver looked like, what time the accident occurred and if they remember the car's number plate. I need to make sure our witnesses are calm and completely prepared before the defence lawyer cross-examines them.

Sarah is a great barrister.

Being cross-examined is when barristers on the opposing side question a witness. This can be a difficult experience for witnesses. They can get flustered and confused when they're on the stand, so it's important to remember that the barristers are just doing their job.

Now what did Daniel see?

Most solicitors in private practice work 45 to 50 hours per week. Many solicitors need to work in the evening or at weekends. For example, solicitors who practise criminal law may be called to assist at police stations at any time of the day or night. The work can involve being under pressure with tight deadlines.

The defence will try to prove that our witnesses are unreliable. They could argue that Clive, the owner of the corner store, was busy with his customers at the time of the accident. He could have been too distracted to notice what type of car hit my client.

The defence could argue that Glenda, who was walking her dog, has bad eyesight so she couldn't be 100% sure what colour the car was or what the driver looked like.

Daniel, the little boy who was playing nearby, might get nervous when he gives his testimony in court. Children can find adults intimidating, so we want to make sure he's as comfortable and confident as possible beforehand.

CONSTRUCTION WORKER CASE

My client and I meet with his former employer and their lawyer. We've asked the employer for a certain amount of money in compensation for my client's injuries, but the employer does not agree to pay. Barrister Matt Graham and I will need to take our case before a judge at the District Court.

Clive runs the corner store. Was he too busy at the time of the crime?

33

There are many popular films about solicitors, their work and what happens in the courtroom. Some are humorous, while others deal with realistic characters and issues.

12 Angry Men

The movie *12 Angry Men* focuses on a jury as they try to reach a verdict for a murder case. The jury must decide whether an 18-year-old Spanish-American is guilty or innocent of murder. At first, the case appears to be straightforward – the defendant has a weak alibi, a knife was left at the murder scene and several witnesses saw the young man running away from the scene. Eleven of the jurors immediately vote that the young man is guilty – only Juror No. 8, Mr. Davis, thinks he is innocent. As the story unfolds, and the jury considers the evidence, their prejudices are exposed.

12 Angry Men

MOVIES

The Firm

In *The Firm*, Tom Cruise plays Mitch McDeere, a young man with a promising future in law. As he is about to sit his Bar exam, a large, successful law firm offers him an attractive deal to come work with them. As the story unfolds, the firm isn't exactly what it appears to be and Mitch is forced to decide between working for them or bringing them to justice.

To Kill a Mockingbird

Based on Harper Lee's prize-winning book, *To Kill a Mockingbird* tells the story of Atticus Finch, a lawyer who lives in Alabama during the 1930s. Though many townspeople try to convince him not to, Atticus agrees to defend an young African-American man falsely charged with a serious crime. Scout, Atticus' daughter, narrates the story as an adult as she remembers her childhood.

Tom Cruise in *The Firm*

To Kill a Mockingbird

Important things to remember

Everyone deserves a fair trial. If someone is charged with a crime, it doesn't automatically mean that they are guilty.

PRESUMPTION OF INNOCENCE — A person charged with a criminal offence is innocent until proven guilty in a court of law.

PROOF BEYOND REASONABLE DOUBT — To convict the accused, the judge or jury has to be satisfied beyond reasonable doubt that the accused committed that crime. It is the prosecution's job to establish the burden of proof. This means they have to convince the judge or the jury that it's almost certain the accused committed the crime.

THE RIGHT TO REMAIN SILENT — An accused person has the right to remain silent. This principle protects the person from self-incrimination.

RULES OF EVIDENCE — These rules determine what evidence can be admitted in court. One important rule is that witnesses can only give evidence about what they heard, saw or experienced directly.

DIDYOUKNOW?

Ridiculous laws

There are some very strange laws in the UK! What about these . . .

- It is illegal to die in the Houses of Parliament.

- It is an act of treason to place a postage stamp bearing the British king or queen's image upside-down.

- Eating mince pies on Christmas Day is banned.

Strange but true

A lady was overjoyed when a DJ on Radio Buxton told her that she had won a car in a quiz competition. But when she arrived at the radio station she was given a 4-inch model of the car! So, she sued and a judge ruled that the radio station had entered into a legally binding contract and ordered them to pay for a real car.

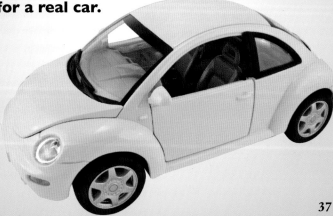

THE VERDICT IS IN

The verdict is in — the hit-and-run case

After three hours, the jury returns with a guilty verdict. The defendant is convicted of dangerous driving and the judge sets a date when he will be sentenced. My client and I are very pleased with this decision, but I suspect the defendant will appeal his verdict at another court.

Update — the pavement injury case

I've arranged to meet Mrs Watson's father now he is at home from hospital. The council who have admitted that the pavement had not been re-laid properly after drainage work. Hopefully they will offer a suitable amount in compensation through an out-of-court settlement.

The court finds you guilty!

The verdict is in — the injured apprentice case

After our court hearing, the judge agrees with us that my client's employer broke workplace health and safety laws. My client had been working without proper equipment which increased the risk of him falling and injuring himself. The judge orders the employer to pay damages in the amount of £6,000.

Jury service

A jury consists of 12 members of the public selected at random. Jurors usually try the more serious criminal cases such as murder, rape, assault, burglary or fraud. These trials take place in the Crown Court. Receiving a jury summons means you are legally required to attend court. Each individual juror will be asked to consider the evidence presented and then decide whether the defendant is guilty or not guilty.

DIDYOUKNOW?

The right of appeal

If the defence or prosecution does not agree with a conviction and/or sentence, they can appeal the case. This means they request that a higher court retry the case.

Back at the office...

A lot of telephone calls and emails await me. I spend the afternoon working on another case and try to respond to as many phone calls as I can.

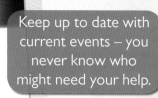

Being a solicitor is a challenging profession. Unfortunately, justice is not always done, but it is important to Keep up the fight. The law protects our rights, our freedom and our security. As a solicitor it's my job to defend clients when a law has been broken, or they are in a position where they cannot defend themselves.

Back on the job!

Keep up to date with current events – you never know who might need your help.

40

Opportunities for solicitors

As a lawyer, you could work in these areas:

- commercial law – work with the big city law firms and advise corporate clients
- local law firm – work for a smaller firm and practise in a wide variety of areas, such as estates, conveyancing and family law
- in-house legal counsel – work for a company and advise them on the law as it affects their business
- Crown Prosecution Service – the government department employs solicitors or barristers as 'crown prosecutors' who ensure that all relevant facts and evidence to support cases are available for the magistrates' courts
- accounting firms – work in the financial industry providing legal expertise to financial transactions

mediate legal disagreements

- legal aid or community legal centre – work for government or non-government legal organisations helping disadvantaged people who can't afford to pay for legal representation
- law reform commissions – help develop government policies and ways to improve the law
- judiciary – work as a magistrate or judge in a court
- education – work as a legal studies teacher
- university – work as a law lecturer and do legal research
- mediation – help disputing parties reach a solution to their disagreement

teach at university

work in legal aid

Follow these steps to become a lawyer

To become a solicitor, you must first meet the necessary academic standards, and then you must complete vocational training.

Getting as much work experience as possible is essential whilst you gain the right qualifications.

In England and Wales, you can get the qualifications by:

- by gaining a qualifying law degree
- by gaining a degree in any other subject, then taking a conversion course – either the Common Professional Examination (CPE) or Graduate Diploma in Law (GDL)
- by qualifying as a Fellow of the Institute of Legal Executives (ILEX)

To pursue a law degree you need top marks in GCSEs/S grades and A/H levels, or alternatives such as an Access to Higher Education qualification. Be realistic – it's one of the most competitive degree courses.

Some universities may ask you to pass the National Admissions Test for Law (LNAT) before accepting you for a degree. Check the exact entry requirements with course providers.

The route to becoming a solicitor in Scotland has different steps. For details check the Lawscot website.

Once you have the qualifications you then need to pass the Legal Practice Course (LPC). You can study the LPC either one year full-time or two years part-time. For details of LPC courses, visit the Law Central Applications Board.

In England and Wales, you then must complete more vocational training by:

- getting a two-year training contract with a firm of solicitors
- passing the Professional Skills Course (PSC) during your training contract.

See the Law Society website for advice about training contracts and the PSC.

Then, when you have fully qualified, you must also take a certain amount of further training and development each year throughout your career. The Law Societies run compulsory continuing professional development (CPD) schemes to help members achieve this.

Other related areas to consider:

Barrister or Advocate (Scotland) – give expert legal advice to professionals employed in positions related to the law and also represent clients in court. Barristers present cases in court and usually specialise in one of several areas.

Court clerk – Her Majesty's Courts Service employs many qualified solicitors and barristers as court clerks (or justices' clerks). Clerks advise lay magistrates on law and procedure, and are involved in the daily running of the courts.

Legal Executive – is able to undertake many of the legal activities that solicitors do. Becoming a legal executive is recognised as being one of the three core ways of becoming a lawyer.

Legal Secretary – provide administrative and secretarial support to those working in the legal profession. They carry out a wide range of administrative and office management duties.

Licensed Conveyancer – is a specialist property lawyer who is trained and qualified in all aspects of the law dealing with property. They advise on the transfer of ownership of property or land.

Paralegal – is a person who performs legal work that requires knowledge of the law and procedures, but who is not a qualified solicitor or barrister. Paralegals may work within a law firm, the public sector or in-house.

Useful contacts

Connexions / Careers Service and UCAS www.ucas.ac.uk

For information on college courses and university degrees, ask your Connexions / Careers Service.

National Admissions Test for Law (LNAT) www.lnat.ac.uk

This website provides full details of the test and application processes.

All About Law – The Law Careers website www.allaboutlaw.co.uk

The Law Careers website provides a full range of information on law careers.

Law Careers www.lawcareers.net

The Law Society www.lawsociety.org.uk

The Law Society website has details about becoming a solicitor.

113 Chancery Lane, London WC2A 1PL Tel: 0870 606 2555

Solicitors Regulation Authority www.sra.org.uk

This website gives loads of information about training.

The Law Society of Scotland www.lawscot.org.uk

For solicitor training and careers in Scotland, this website is a great resource.

Institute of Legal Executives www.ilex.org.uk

Looks at every aspect of a career as a legal executive.

Institute of Legal Secretaries www.institutelegalsecretaries.com

Guidance on legal secretary careers and training.

The National Association of Licensed Paralegals

www.nationalparalegals.com

Look here for information on paralegal qualifications and training.

Glossary

alibi – a form of defense where the accused person claims or proves that they were somewhere else at the time that a crime was committed

compensation – an amount of money or something else given to pay for loss, damage or work done

counsel – a lawyer or group of lawyers who present cases in court or give legal advice

custody – the legal right and responsibility of raising a child

damages – money paid as compensation

ethical – accepted principles of behaviour that are thought to be right

FBI – Federal Bureau of Investigation; part of the U.S. Justice Department that deals with matters of national security, interstate crime and crimes against the government

fraud – a crime where someone deceives someone else, usually for financial gain

humanities – the study of subjects such as literature, language, history and philosophy

judiciary – a country's court system and/or group of judges

manslaughter – the unlawful killing of someone by accident

monarch – a king or queen, who rules a State or territory

Prohibition – a period of time during the 1920s and 1930s in North America when it was illegal to make, transport and sell alcohol

self-incrimination – when what you say or how you act suggests that you are guilty, especially during court testimony

sole practitioner – somebody who works in a profession, on their own

sue – to take legal action against somebody to obtain something, usually compensation for a wrong

testimony – written or spoken evidence that a witness gives in court

unanimous – agreed on by everyone

voluntarily – arising, acting, or resulting from somebody's own choice or decision rather than from external pressure or force

Index

WHAT'S IT LIKE TO BE A...? **PILOT**
Elizabeth Dowen · Lisa Thompson

WHAT'S IT LIKE TO BE A...? **FORENSIC SCIENTIST**
Elizabeth Dowen · Lisa Thompson

WHAT'S IT LIKE TO BE A...? **TV PRODUCER**
Elizabeth Dowen · Lisa Thompson

WHAT'S IT LIKE TO BE A...? **MAGAZINE EDITOR**
Elizabeth Dowen · Lisa Thompson

WHAT'S IT LIKE TO BE A...? **GAME DEVELOPER**
Elizabeth Dowen · Lisa Thompson

WHAT'S IT LIKE TO BE A...? **MOTOR MECHANIC**
Elizabeth Dowen · Lisa Thompson

WHAT'S IT LIKE TO BE A...? **ANIMATOR**
Elizabeth Dowen · Lisa Thompson

WHAT'S IT LIKE TO BE A...? **BUILDER**
Elizabeth Pickard · Lisa Thompson

WHAT'S IT LIKE TO BE A...? **CHEF**
Elizabeth Pickard · Lisa Thompson

WHAT'S IT LIKE TO BE A...? **SPORTS TRAINER**
Elizabeth Dowen · Lisa Thompson

WHAT'S IT LIKE TO BE A...? **FASHION DESIGNER**
Elizabeth Pickard · Lisa Thompson

WHAT'S IT LIKE TO BE A...? **CHOREOGRAPHER**
Elizabeth Dowen · Lisa Thompson